Injalak Arts & Crafts Association
is an Aboriginal-owned and -governed community
organization based in Gunbalanya, West Arnhem Land,
in the Northern Territory of Australia.
Founded in 1989, it numbers over two hundred artists
and craftspeople—male and female, young and old.

www.enchantedlion.com

First published in 2022 by Enchanted Lion Books,
248 Creamer Street, Studio 4, Brooklyn, NY 11231

Text copyright © 2022 by Felicity Wright
Illustrations copyright © 2022 by Gabriel Maralngurra
Editors: Lawrence Kim, Emilie Robert Wong, and Claudia Bedrick

A CIP record is on file with the Library of Congress

ISBN 978-1-59270-356-2

Book design: Jonathan Yamakami

Printed in China by RR Donnelley Asia Printing Solutions Ltd.

First Printing

A KUNWINJKU COUNTING BOOK

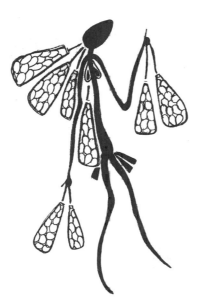

Gabriel Maralngurra
and Felicity Wright

Paintings by Gabriel Maralngurra

Enchanted Lion Books
NEW YORK

Preface

West Arnhem Land, in the Northern Territory of Australia, is home to the Bininj, an Indigenous people who speak a language called Kunwinjku. The contemporary paintings that follow depict some of the many reptiles, birds, insects, fish, and other creatures that live in this ecologically complex region. They are inspired by rock art that is thousands of years old.

1

One crocodile with many sharp teeth

Nakudji kinga kakarrme kunyidme

Saltwater or estuarine crocodile • *Kinga*

Kinga are found along the coast of northern Australia, on beaches and in estuarine rivers and billabongs (isolated ponds left behind after a river changes course). They live in both salt water and fresh water. Freshwater kinga are almost black, far darker than those living in salt water.

Kinga cannot breathe or swallow when underwater. They have a flap of skin that closes off their throat while they're immersed. This prevents water from coming in, even with their mouth open. They either catch their prey while submerged and jump out of the water to eat, or they attack on land.

From November to March, when the rains start, kinga mate. They make big nests in the long grass or in forest areas close to rivers, billabongs, and waterholes.

Today, when Bininj people go into the water where kinga live, we sing songs to keep ourselves safe. Our ancestors, however, had ceremonial scars on their bodies that frightened kinga away.

In West Arnhem Land, we eat kinga, but people in central and northeastern Arnhem Land do not because of their *djang* (creation stories and ceremonies) and accompanying beliefs.

2 Two snake-necked turtles swimming in a billabong

Ngalmangiyi bokenh kabenedjuhme kore kulabbarl

Northern snake-necked turtle • *Ngalmangiyi*

Ngalmangiyi always live on floodplains, close to fresh water. They are strong swimmers. Like sea turtles, ngalmangiyi lay their eggs in mud. The buried eggs hatch in March or April.

During *kudjewk* (wet season), ngalmangiyi eat as many tadpoles, frogs, and fish as they can, getting really fat. Then, they bury themselves in the mud and hibernate until the rains begin again.

Women hunting for ngalmangiyi will look for *mim* (small holes through which the turtles breathe while buried underground). Hunters poke through the mud with a digging stick that has a sharpened point called a *kunbarlkbu*. If the stick makes a knocking sound, there is sure to be a turtle there.

Ngalmangiyi are delicious. We cook them whole, either over a fire or in a *kunkerri* (ground oven). Afterwards, we often paint the shells.

3 Three water goannas soaking up the sun

Danjbik burarr kabirri kukdayo

Mertens' water monitor or goanna • *Burrar*

This reptile loves water. During the day, it can be found basking in the sun on rocks and logs on the banks of rivers, creeks, and billabongs. If approached, it will quickly slither away or drop into the water to hide. The nostrils on the top of its head allow it to breathe while submerged.

It eats small water creatures, such as frogs, fish, crabs, and certain mammals. It also forages on land for small mammals, birds, eggs, and even insects.

Burrar are tasty. Their eggs are good to eat, too.

We are worried about the future of burrar because of the harmful spread of cane toads, which—ironically—were originally introduced into Australia to control pests. If burrar eat these poisonous toads, they will die.

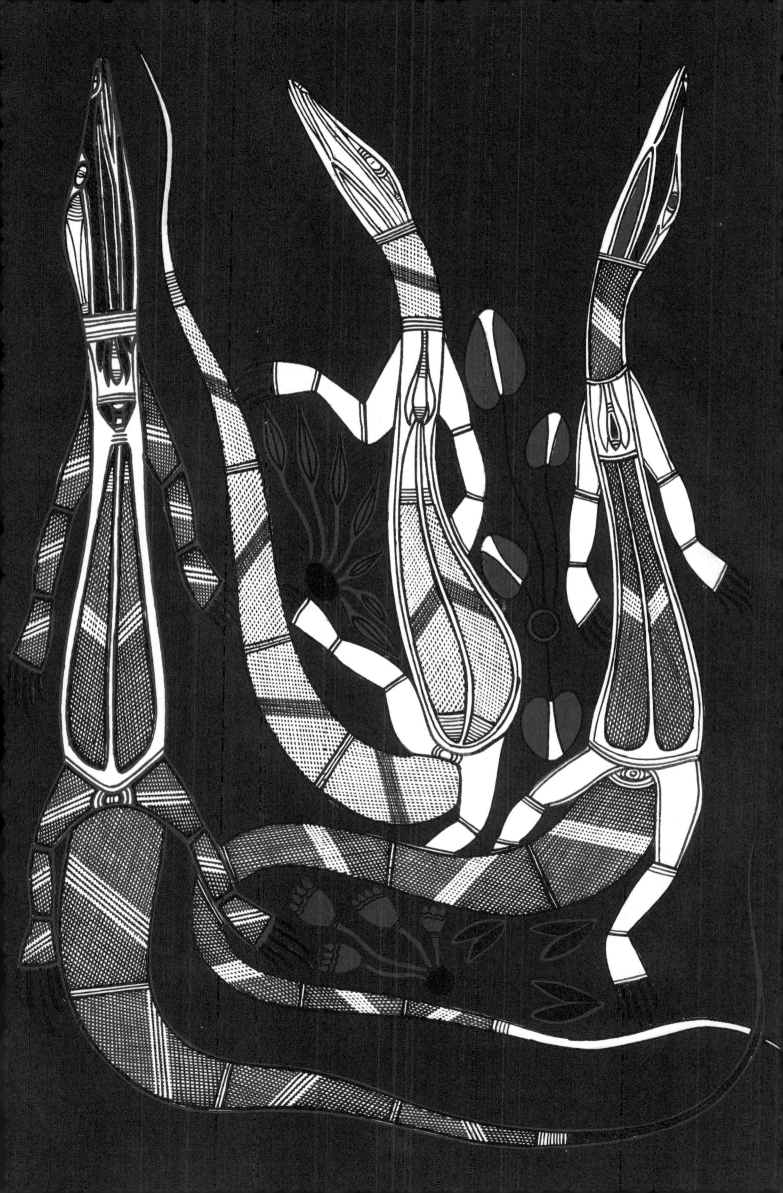

4 Four spoonbills standing on the floodplain

Kunkarrngbakmeng kebbalhdjurri kabirrihni kore kabbal

Royal spoonbill • *Kebbalhdjurri*

Kebbalhdjurri are large white birds with black bills. They love floodplains and billabongs and like to visit the Adjumarllarl Billabong in Gunbalanya (a large Aboriginal community in West Arnhem Land) in the early dry season. Here, we see two males (top) and two females (bottom).

Kebbalhdjurri have very long legs and large, flat bills. They eat by wading through shallow water and sweeping their partially opened bills from side to side. The moment a tiny fish, crustacean, mollusk, or water insect touches the inside of the bill, it snaps shut. These birds need to feed for many hours and do so during both day and night.

Kebbalhdjurri nest in trees. The male gathers reeds and sticks, and the female uses this material to weave together a large, shallow bowl or platform. She then lays, on average, a clutch of three smooth, oval, white eggs. Each parent takes turns incubating the eggs.

Our ancestors hunted them for food with spears and sticks. Today, we still eat them occasionally (they taste a lot like chicken).

5 Five agile wallabies eating leaves

Kunbidkudji kornobolo karbirringun kunworr

Agile wallaby • *Kornobolo*

Kornobolo live in woodlands and swamps all over West Arnhem Land and neighboring Kakadu. You may even see them on the side of the road. They mainly feed at night on grasses, legumes, and other herbaceous plants, but they also forage by day, especially during the wet season.

We call the male *warradjangkal* and the female *merlbbe*. We also call them *njamdjorrhdjorrh*, which means "get a big belly," because they're so delicious that people find them hard to resist!

When hunting kornobolo, we often use a grass fire to flush out all the animals in one direction. In the old days, people hunted them using *mankole* (spears) and *borndok* (spear throwers). They would smear *delek* (white clay) under their armpits and hold a branch in front of themselves so that the wallaby couldn't smell them or see them approaching.

In Kunwinjku sign language, the sign for kornobolo is an open-handed chopping motion. This imitates the wallaby's tail hitting the ground. Wallabies do this to trick predators into thinking they have moved when, in fact, they are hiding in the same place.

6

Six echidnas inside an anthill

Kunbidkudji dja mankudji ngarrbek karribirrni kore kunboy

Short-beaked echidna • *Ngarrbek*

In Arnhem Land, *ngarrbek* live in woodlands and the Stone Country (a sandstone plateau in Arnhem Land known for its sheer cliffs, deep gorges, and spectacular waterfalls). They are covered in fur and have spines like a hedgehog. When frightened, these animals roll themselves up into balls to protect their soft belly and heart.

Ngarrbek have extremely strong front limbs and very sharp claws, which allow them to burrow quickly and tear apart termite nests. Although they usually walk slowly, they can stretch out and run as fast as a dog. They dislike heat, so they often sleep and rest during the day.

Ngarrbek have no teeth and cannot bite or chew. Instead, they suck up ants and termites through a long, bony beak. Despite this strange diet, they are delicious to eat, with a taste like emu, which is beefy in flavor.

Our ancestors would search for them on nights when the moon was bright enough for hunting. Their dogs would find ngarrbek by smell.

7 Seven dragonflies resting on flowers

Kunbidkudji dja bokenh djalangkarridj-djalangkarridj kabirribarndi kore mannguy

Dragonfly • *Djalangkarridj-djalangkarridj*
Many different species of dragonflies are found in West Arnhem Land. *Djalangkarridj-djalangkarridj* is the generic Kunwinjku name for these insects. They are very social and form beautiful dancing, darting swarms.

Dragonflies are indicators of seasonal change. One kind tells us when *kudjewk* (the wet season) has ended and *bangkerreng* (the early dry season) has begun. The appearance of another, bigger kind of dragonfly lets us know that *yekke* (the cold dry season) has arrived.

When our ancestors saw a dragonfly in February or March, they would say, "The fish are ready to be caught!" Then, they would go to a billabong, or to a small creek running into the sea, where they knew there would be good fishing.

Arnhem Land is home to many thousands of insect species, which all play a role in the ecosystem, especially as food for other creatures. The great variety of insects here is due to the varied habitats and relatively high temperatures throughout the year.

Eight water pythons slithering in the mud

Kunbidkudji dja danjbik borlokko karribirri wake kukih

Water python • *Borlokko*

Borlokko are large snakes that are plentiful in and around fresh water. They are nocturnal and feed on a variety of animals, including waterbirds and their eggs. Young borlokko eat frogs, fish, and lizards.

We hunt for borlokko by searching for them in the water with our hands. They have small, sharp teeth, but they aren't venomous.

They are able to catch and swallow prey larger than themselves by dislocating their jaw. They can even eat *kulubarn* (fruit bats). When we see a lump inside of them, we know they have just eaten something big.

Their meat is white and tastes a bit like chicken. Duwa people (one group of Bininj) cannot eat borlokko because of their religious beliefs, but Yirridjdja people (another group) can.

9 Nine snapping turtles eating bugs

Kunbidkudji dja kunkarrngbakmeng ngarderrhwo kabirringun dumdum

Northern snapping turtle • *Ngarderrhwo*

Ngarderrhwo live in freshwater rivers and waterholes. We warn our children, "Don't pick it up! Don't touch it!" because if you put your finger in its mouth, it might snap shut, and the razor-sharp teeth will cut off your finger!

These short-necked turtles are distinct from *ngalmangiyi* (snake-necked turtles) and *warradjan* (pig-nosed turtles).

This turtle buries its eggs on land. They hatch around the same time as those of ngalmangiyi. We eat ngarderrhwo, as well as the other two kinds of turtles. They all taste good.

10

Ten knob-tailed geckos crawling on the ground

Kunbidkudji bokenh boywek kabirriwake kore kungarre

Prickly knob-tailed gecko • *Boywek*

Boywek are knob-tailed geckos that have rough or prickly skin. They live among rocks, where their camouflage makes them hard to see. They are close relatives of the Asian geckos that many people keep as pets. Unlike their cousins, boywek do not have suckers on their feet. Instead, they have sharp claws that they use to climb.

These reptiles are the push-up kings of geckos. They do push-ups when they feel threatened to make themselves look tougher and more intimidating. One of their favorite things to do is fighting one another. And if one happens to lose its tail, another simply grows back to take its place!

When it comes to food, boywek are not fussy eaters. Almost any suitably sized insect will do. As for us, we do not consider boywek food and do not eat them, as they are far too small!

11

Eleven freshwater prawns swimming in a creek

Kunbidkudji kunbidkudji dja mankudji wakih kabirri djuhme kore kukabo

Freshwater prawn • *Wakih*

Wakih is a kind of river prawn or freshwater shrimp that lives in permanent upland streams. They are found only in West Arnhem Land and Kakadu.

Gagadjui, the scientific species name of this shellfish, is derived from *Gagudju*, the Indigenous name for the language and people of Kakadu.

We catch wakih in billabongs and the deep parts of waterholes. We usually hunt for them at night using a throw net, or by luring them with a piece of raw meat at the end of a fishing line into the shallows, where they can be speared.

Our ancestors used *walabi* (a net consisting of the fibrous roots of young boab trees strung on a triangular wooden frame) or *madjabu* (fish traps) baited with raw meat or raw *mankindjek* (a type of yam) to catch wakih.

Our ancestors went after wakih so eagerly because they taste so good!

12 Twelve barramundi swimming upstream

Kunbidkudji kunbidkudji dja bokenh namarnkorl kabirri djuhme kore mankabo

Barramundi • *Namarnkorl*

Namarnkorl (barramundi) is a type of fish that lives in fresh water, salt water, and estuaries. We refer to this fish by different names depending on its age: *marlarlak* for juveniles and *birlmu* for adults.

Namarnkorl spawn during the full moon. Their iridescent skin can be seen shimmering in the water during their mating dance.

The best time of the year for catching namarnkorl is *bangkerreng* (the early dry season in March and April), after *kudjewk* (the wet season). We use a lure on a fishing line to catch namarnkorl. Our ancestors would use a *walabi* (fish net) or a *djalakirradj* (Macassan-style pronged spear).

We cook the fish whole in a ground oven or over coals. We use *mankorrko* (known as melaleuca or paperbark) to add a special herb flavor. We also use this bark when cooking kangaroo and buffalo.

An Ancient Tradition

The Indigenous people of West Arnhem Land refer to themselves as Bininj, meaning simply people. The Bininj are subdivided into various cultural groups, all of which speak Kunwinjku. Within these groups, all artists, for example, belong to a particular *kunmokurrkurr* (clan), which influences the *djang* (ancestral creation stories or dreamings) and other stories that they are allowed to represent. Every clan has a *kunred*, which is a specific area of the country they identify as home.

Many of the images and graphic techniques used in contemporary Bininj art are based on those found in the hundreds of ancient rock art galleries and bark shelters scattered across West Arnhem Land. Some of the paintings found on Injalak Hill are over 15,000 years old.

Since the beginning of time, the Bininj people have used rock art—along with dance, music, and oral storytelling—to express and pass down ancestral beliefs, traditions, and laws. Across time, rock art has been used in both secular and sacred ways. As regards daily life, it is used to design fabrics and ceramics, decorate the home, and to tell and illustrate stories and train new artists. It also plays a significant role in specifically ceremonial contexts, where the formal transmission of sacred knowledge takes place.

Tools and Techniques

Ancient Bininj art had its own set of artistic principles and tools.
Contemporary artists still draw on these traditions to create new works.

Milhbarung (painting the background) is the first step.

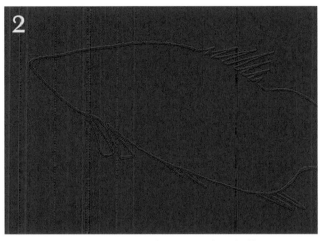

Next, the artist paints the *waralno* (silhouette of the figure). *Waralno* also means shadow, or spirit; some believe that ancestral beings place their spirit in the painting in the form of a picture (*waralkurrmerrinj*).

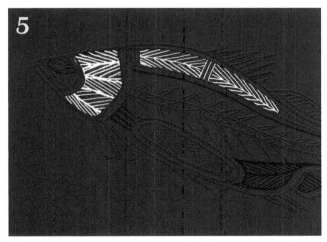

At this stage, the internal organs of an animal are often depicted. This is known as x-ray style.

Details like *rarrk* (hatching—a technique that creates tonal or shading effects) are then added. In rock paintings, these are usually parallel lines in red ochre.

Many contemporary artworks feature complex crosshatching in red, yellow, black, and white, a style that originated in ceremonial painting.

The *rarrk* painted by the Yirridjdja (one group of Bininj) are fine, whereas those of the Duwa (another group) are thicker. Fine *rarrk* are painted with a *manyilk*, which is a brush made from sedge (a grass-like plant). The stalk of the sedge is shaved down until only a few fibers remain. Larger brush strokes are traditionally made with a *kerlkbak*, which is a brush fashioned from strips of stringybark (a type of eucalyptus tree).

Seasons in Kunwinjku

JAN-FEB: *KUDJEWK*
The wet season. The monsoon brings heavy rains and high winds. Fireflies appear, signaling that the abundant bush fruits are ready to be picked.

NOV-DEC: *KUNUMELENG*
Humidity builds. Clouds and wind gather from all directions. There is a lot of thunder and lightning.

MAR-APR: *BANGKERRENG*
The early dry season. Powerful "knock 'em down storms" flatten the grass. This is the moment to collect magpie goose eggs and a good time for fishing.

The lives of all the creatures in this book are closely tied to the seasons of West Arnhem Land. The Bininj divide the year into six seasons:

SEP-OCT: *KURRUNG*
The hot dry season. The air is fragrant with the scent of flowers. It's a good time to hunt magpie geese, long-necked turtles, and file snakes.

JULY-AUG: *WURRKENG*
The cool weather season. Many plants flower. The bees are busy, so it's a good time to collect sugarbag (a type of honey).

MAY-JUNE: *YEKKE*
The cold dry season. The rains are over; cooler temperatures and northeasterly winds have arrived. Dragonflies and Kimberley heather appear. Kapok trees flower.

Gabriel Maralngurra

"I wanted to paint for schoolkids. When they go to school, they don't know how to count in Kunwinjku. If a Bininj child reads this book, I hope they will learn about Bininj culture and how to count in Kunwinjku."

Gabriel Maralngurra was born on July 18, 1968, in Gunbalanya. He is a member of the Ngalngbali clan. His clan estate (his father's father's homeland) is Kudjekbinj, northeast of Gunbalanya. Gabriel co-founded Injalak Arts in 1989 and continues to be a driving force behind the center today in his role as co-manager.

His confident and fluid style is unmistakable, always balancing studied naturalism with a strong sense of design and stylization. His work references the ancient rock art of West Arnhem Land but also pursues formal innovations and new designs. He particularly enjoys painting billabong scenes featuring freshwater animals, as well Kudjekbinj *djang* (creation stories), involving Wurdyaw Djang (an important sacred site), mermaids, rainbow serpents, and crocodiles.

In addition to ochre or acrylic paintings on watercolor paper, Gabriel creates paintings on bark and canvas and makes designs for screen printing on fabric. He also makes images through linocuts and copper-plate etching.

He is now an ambassador for Bininj culture, having worked for many years as a fabric screen printer and designer, tour guide, Kunwinjku-English translator, and Injalak Arts board member and chairperson. He has traveled widely around Australia and internationally for art-related events.

Why did you choose to paint the images you did for this book?
I chose to paint these images because I like painting. Each of these animals means something to me; plus, they are good to eat all year-round.

Is there a creature you especially enjoy painting?
I just paint what's in my head—I like all of them!

What made you start painting? Why do you continue to paint?
I used to watch all the old men paint at Injalak Arts; they told me stories about the creation ancestors. I was inspired by these old men. And then, I just like painting. Now I teach younger men how to paint and about Bininj art, cross-hatching, and rock art style.

What inspired you to create this book? What effect do you hope the book will have?
I wanted to paint for schoolkids. When they go to school, they don't know how to count in Kunwinjku. If a Bininj child reads this book, I hope they will learn about Bininj culture and how to count in Kunwinjku.

It's not just for Australians, but also for people overseas to learn about Bininj culture, animal names in Kunwinjku, how Bininj people catch these animals and in what months, how we cook them, and also where they live. I want people all over the world to learn something about Bininj culture and maybe come over and visit Gunbalanya and Injalak Arts.

A Note on Pronunciation

<u>VOWELS</u>
a as in <u>a</u>bout, b<u>u</u>t
e as in b<u>e</u>d or French è
i as in b<u>i</u>t
o as in p<u>o</u>t or Italian o (as in *Di<u>o</u>*)
u as in p<u>u</u>t

<u>DIPHTHONGS</u>
aw as in h<u>ou</u>se
ay as in "<u>aye aye</u>, captain"
ew (no English equivalent—e of b<u>e</u>d shortly
    followed by u of p<u>u</u>t)
ey as in h<u>ey</u>, th<u>ey</u>
iw (no English equivalent—i of b<u>i</u>t shortly
    followed by u of p<u>u</u>t)
oy as in b<u>oy</u>
ow as in <u>oa</u>k, ch<u>o</u>ke
uy (no English equivalent—nearest to oy of b<u>oy</u>,
    as in Australian township Nhulunb<u>uy</u>)

<u>CONSONANTS</u>
b as in <u>b</u>ank
d as in <u>d</u>og
dj as in <u>j</u>ump
h as in u<u>h</u>-oh
k as in <u>g</u>et
l as in <u>l</u>eaf
m as in <u>m</u>ad
n as in <u>n</u>ose
ng as in si<u>ng</u>
nj as in ca<u>ny</u>on
r as in <u>r</u>ice
rr as in American pronunciation of bu<u>tt</u>er
rd as in American pronunciation of ha<u>rd</u>er
rl as in American pronunciation of Ha<u>rl</u>em
rn as in American pronunciation of ha<u>rn</u>ess
w as in <u>w</u>ait
y as in <u>y</u>ell

Long consonants are written double, e.g., bb, dd,
djdj, kk, rdd. These have no English equivalent.

Felicity Wright

Felicity Wright grew up in Melbourne.
Since 1986, she has been living and working
in rural and remote places, mainly with
Indigenous Australian artists. She describes
her work, which is also her passion, as
intercultural mediation.

Acknowledgements

Thanks to:
• The Australian Department of Sustainability,
  Environment, Water, Population and
  Communities (DSEWPaC)
• The Australian Department of the Environment
• Daniel Kennedy
• Dr. Luke Taylor
• John Woinarski, Parks & Wildlife Commission
  of the Northern Territory
• Emma Ligtermoet, Commonwealth Scientific and
  Industrial Research Organisation (CSIRO), Land
  and Water, Darwin, Northern Territory

*Enchanted Lion Books would like to thank
Sallie Lowenstein for introducing this book to us.*